THE ESSENTIAL HEGEL

THE
ESSENTIAL
HEGEL

Paul Strathern

TED SMART

This edition first published in Great Britain in 2003 by
Virgin Books Ltd
Thames Wharf Studios
Rainville Road
London
W6 9HA

First published in the USA in 1997 as *Hegel in 90 Minutes* by Ivan R Dee

This book produced for The Book People Ltd,
Hall Wood Avenue, Haydock, St Helens, WA11 9UL

ISBN 0 7535 0979 2

Typeset by TW Typesetting, Plymouth, Devon
Printed and bound in Great Britain by
Clays Ltd, St Ives PLC

CONTENTS

INTRODUCTION

In 1770, the year of Hegel's birth, Kant delivered his inaugural dissertation at the University of Königsberg. In the same year the poets Hölderlin and Wordsworth were born. The seeds of ecstatic lyricism and profoundly sober systemisation were sown: the extremes of subjectivity and objectivity. Europe stood on the brink of its greatest transformation since the Renaissance. The French Revolution was the political manifestation of this change; the Romantic Movement was its cultural expression.

Meanwhile the Industrial Revolution was to change the face of the entire continent. And within years of Hegel's death, Marx was preparing a further transformation which was to change the face of the twentieth century.

Hegel was to be profoundly involved in both these transformations. In a U-turn such as could only have been encompassed by his celebrated dialectical method, the student Hegel welcomed the French Revolution, and the aged Hegel sang the praises of the arch-conservative Prussian state.

In the hands of Hegel, the dialectical method produced the most elephantine philosophical system known to man, a monolith in praise of the monolithic state. Yet in the hands of his avid follower Marx, Hegel's method was to produce the greatest revolution since the French Revolution, which in its turn produced the most elephantine political system known to man (which in many aspects bore an uncanny resemblance to the Prussian state). This was much how Hegel's dialectical system was meant to work, though he probably wouldn't have seen it this way.

HEGEL'S LIFE AND WORKS

'The height of audacity in serving up pure nonsense, in stringing together senseless and extravagant mazes of words, such as had previously only been known in madhouses, was finally reached in Hegel, and became the instrument of the most barefaced general mystification that has ever taken place, with a result which will appear fabulous to posterity, and will remain as a monument to German stupidity.' So wrote Schopenhauer, who was Hegel's colleague at the University of Berlin. This remark is not intended to prejudice but merely to warn. With Hegel, philosophy becomes a matter of *extreme seriousness*, so we'd best get any jokes out of the way right at the start. As an earnest English hellfire preacher of the period commented while delivering a sermon to an amused fashionable audience in Bath, 'There's no hope for them that laughs.'

With Hegel, philosophy became very difficult indeed, requiring the *utmost concentration*. So it looks as if Schopenhauer, despite his razorsharp intellect, just wasn't trying hard enough. On the other hand, even Hegel conceded that 'only one man understands me, and even he does not'. Some critics consider that here Hegel was exaggerating. Did this man ever really exist?

Georg Wilhelm Friedrich Hegel was born on 27 August, in Stuttgart. His family had for generations been civil servants, and his father worked in the Württemberg tax office. Hegel's upbringing gave him a heavy Swabian accent which he retained to the end of his days, as well as the belief that self-effacement is one of the cardinal virtues of true culture.

He was a sickly child and was to suffer from several bouts of serious illness before he reached manhood. At the age of six he caught such a bad case of smallpox that he nearly died. For more than a week he was blinded, and his complexion remained badly pockmarked. At the age of eleven he survived the fever that struck his entire family and carried off his mother. And during his student years he was laid low for several months by a malarial infection.

As Hegel grew up he read omnivorously – through literature, newspapers, and treatises on almost any subject he could find. Yet even at an early age he already believed in a strictly systematic approach, meticulously copying out in his journals excerpts from all he read. This thorough training in pedantry (his 'excerpt mill', as he called it) contained quotations on everything, from physiognomy to philosophy, from hyperboreans to hypochondria. Personal matters were included in this journal only when they illuminated an abstract principle. And on days when he found nothing serious enough to record, Hegel took this seriously enough to record why such a lamentable state of affairs had occurred. Avid scholarly readers of this junk shop of the mind may come across side by side a report of a local fire and a criticism of a concert he has attended, followed by a description and analysis of the cold weather, a brief treatise on the homily 'Love of money is the root of all evil', and a list of the merits he has discerned in the Latin dictionary he has just received as a present. One scholarly reader notes: 'He composes a Latin oration, he argues against dictating a theme in German for transcription into Latin, he puts down his school timetable in the margin, he says that he and his friends watched pretty girls, he makes notes on Virgil and Demosthenes, he is curious about a musical clock and a star atlas, and on Sunday he works on trigonometry.'

It is difficult to overemphasise the importance of this 'excerpt mill' – as an illustration both of exceptional learning and of premature desiccation. In later life Hegel's mammoth tomes were to contain references to an almost superhuman breadth of learning. The fact that these references often contained minor errors only confirms the encyclopaedic volume of Hegel's mind. They were invariably quoted from memory – Hegel was averse to interrupting his train of thought by looking up sources or checking quotations.

Hegel's father was 'a man of orderly habits and the conservative instincts natural to his place', according to Hegel's early biographer Caird. This archetypical employee of the provincial tax office appears to have been a somewhat distant father. Hegel's closest human contact during this period was his sister Christiane, who was three years his junior. The motherless pair developed a strong affection for each other. The abstract principle that Hegel elicited from this rare personal emotion was that a sister's love for her brother is the highest form of love. In his later philosophy he was to illustrate this by citing Sophocles' *Antigone*, in which the dutiful Antigone is willing to face death in order to bury her brother's corpse, and then commits suicide, an act that results in further suicides and desolation. As we shall see, the charged atmosphere of this Greek tragedy mirrored the underlying psychological truth of the relationship between Hegel and his sister. The impressionable Christiane was overwhelmed by her all-knowing brother, and her love for him developed into an unnaturally strong bond which was to have tragic consequences.

At the age of eighteen Hegel enrolled in the theological seminary at Tübingen University. Although he exhibited all the characteristics of a first-class civil servant, his family wanted him to enter the church. Hegel's interests already extended far beyond theology, but it wasn't until he entered the university that he first became seriously interested in philosophy. It was this interest that brought him into contact with two exceptional contemporaries at Tübingen. One was Hölderlin, an ardent Hellenophile, who was to become one of the outstanding lyric poets in the German language; the other was Schelling, whose intensely romantic philosophy of nature was a forerunner of the nineteenth-century reaction against the shallow constrictions of rationalism. In such heady company, Hegel soon became a romantic revolutionary. When the French Revolution exploded, he and Schelling rose at dawn to plant a 'Tree of Liberty' in the marketplace.

Hegel became deeply interested in ancient Greek culture and the new philosophy of Kant. The publication of Kant's *Critique of Pure Reason*, just seven years earlier in 1781, was hailed by Hegel as the 'greatest event in the entire history of German philosophy'.

To appreciate why Kant was so important, it is necessary to outline the previous history of philosophy. In the mid-eighteenth century the Scottish philosopher Hume had reduced philosophic certainty to its lowest ebb. Experience, he declared, was our only source of true knowledge. Hume's empirical philosophy had demonstrated the impossibility of creating any further philosophical systems. To build any system one needed such elements as causality (that is, cause and effect), but Hume had shown that this was a mere supposition. No one had ever experienced a cause and its ensuing effect; all they had actually experienced was one thing following another. It looked as if this was the end of philosophy.

Kant, however, managed to circumvent this catastrophe. He suggested that causality was merely one of the ways in which we apprehend the world – like space and time, colour, and so forth. Hume had been right: the world didn't contain such a thing as causality, instead it was in us, our way of perceiving the world.

Building on this foundation, Kant managed to construct by means of reason an all-embracing philosophical system that explained everything. In a series of all but impenetrable works, Kant proceeded to explain his system to the world. The great era of German metaphysics was launched in all its high-mindedness and prolixity. Hegel was enraptured: here was a mind as encyclopaedic (and prosaic) as his own.

Hegel ploughed assiduously through Kant, complementing this with forays into ancient Greek culture, and in between times harvesting far and wide for the 'excerpt mill'. Even in these early years he was known by his fellow students as 'the old man', apparently as much for his drab personality as his obsessive propensity for study. By the time Hegel came to leave the university in 1793, he had no intention of entering the church. What he really wanted was an academic post, teaching in a university, but surprisingly he managed to achieve only a mediocre degree. His final certificate from the university authorities perceptively noted that he was not much good at philosophy.

In fact Hegel's reading, in philosophy and other subjects, had been almost exclusively outside his course – the mark of many a brilliant mind and countless mediocrities. Hegel was intent on continuing with these whimsical studies, and in order to support himself he became a private tutor. This took him to Berne in Switzerland for three years. Here he read widely in the library and was quite lonely. He found solace by communing with nature.

His response to the spectacular local Alpine scenery provides a curious psychological picture. 'I seek to be reconciled with myself, and with other men, in the arms of Nature', he wrote. 'For this reason I often fly to this true mother, to isolate myself from other men in her company. She enables me to protect myself from them, and prevent any covenant with them.' Yet for him the sublime Alpine peaks were 'eternally dead' while he saw a waterfall as the very image of freedom and play, eternally moving forward. The psychologist Scharfstein has suggested that the bleak mountain peaks evoked for Hegel 'the painful immobility of depression' and that the waterfall represented 'the pleasure of release from it'. Whether or not this represents psychological insight or interpretive overkill, Hegel certainly suffered from severe bouts of depression during this period, an affliction that probably lasted throughout his life. (Both his prose and his portraits would seem to confirm this.)

Under the influence of his hero Kant, Hegel now wrote a number of religious treatises critical of Christian authoritarianism, and a *Life of Christ* which treated Jesus as an almost wholly secular figure. In this work Jesus' explanations of Christian doctrine often bear an uncanny resemblance to the words of Hegel's hero – the Galilean's profound simplicities undergoing a painful transformation into the serpentine ponderousness of Prussian philosophising. Kant had based his moral philosophy upon his so-called categorical imperative: 'One should act only in accordance with such a maxim as one would simultaneously will should become a universal law.' This plainly derives from Jesus' 'Do unto others, as unto yourself.' Hegel's game attempt to emulate Kant ended up with Christ saying, 'What you can will to be a universal law among men, and also hold as a law for yourself, according to that maxim you should act.' Hegel's version of Jesus was down to earth in both style and content, a spiritless transmogrification which he came to regret. (This book was never published in his lifetime, and in later years he attempted to destroy all copies of it.)

In 1796 his friend Hölderlin secured him a tutoring job in Frankfurt, where the poet was living at the time. But when Hegel arrived he found that Hölderlin was deliriously in love with a banker's wife whom he believed to be the incarnation of ancient Greece, and once again Hegel found himself on his own. In order to distract himself from his increasing melancholia, Hegel studied even harder. During the little free time he allowed himself, he began composing excruciatingly depressive poems in ill-constructed meter:

'A wise law forbad poorer spirits from making known
what he in holy night has seen, heard, and felt
so that his higher self be not disturbed in contemplation by their noisy nonsense,
so that their twaddle not provoke his anger towards Holiness itself,
so that the Holy not be trodden so in dirt . . .'

Hegel's forte was ever the prosaic, despite his equivocal attitude towards 'noisy nonsense' and 'twaddle'.

In the midst of these solitary years Hegel experienced some sort of profound mystic vision. This appears to have been in the form of an insight into the divine unity of the cosmos, where all finite division was seen as illusory, everything was interdependent, and the ultimate reality was the whole. Hegel had been reading the seventeenth-century Jewish pantheist Spinoza during this period, and Spinoza's philosophy seems to have greatly influenced this vision.

Spinoza's system was in many ways as daunting as Kant's. It was constructed in the style of Euclidian geometry. Starting out from a few basic axioms and definitions, it proceeded by a series of theorems to build up an infinite system of extreme purity and rationalism. This universe-as-geometrical-system was God, and He alone was completely real. He (and thus the infinite universe of which He consisted) contained no negation and was ruled by absolute logical necessity, as in Spinoza's proofs. The negative, evil, finite, and accidental world seen by humanity was due to our nature as finite beings who were unable to grasp the absolute necessity and true reality of the infinite whole.

As a result of his Spinozistic vision, Hegel decided to abandon such distractions as poetry, blasphemy, and keeping a diary in the form of an encyclopaedia. Instead he would devote himself entirely to philosophy. From now on Hegel was to spend the rest of his life articulating his mystic vision of the cosmos and giving it a rational intellectual basis. The result would be his own all-embracing system.

From the outset this system was to bear many resemblances to Spinoza's – apart, of course, from geometric clarity. When it came to presentation, Hegel still favoured the Kantian approach: monumental obfuscation. But it was Spinoza who had shown Hegel how to break free of Kant's overwhelming influence. Kant's was not the only possible philosophic system.

In 1799 Hegel's father died, and he was left a small inheritance – $1,500, according to Durrant, which means it may have been 1,500 thalers (from which the word dollar derives). Hegel now had just enough to live on, and he wrote to his friend Schelling asking if he could recommend a German city where Hegel could live cheaply – one with a simple local cuisine, a comprehensive library, and 'ein gutes bier' (a drinkable draft). At the time Schelling was the precocious star professor of the University of Jena, and he immediately encouraged

Hegel to join him. (Unusually for philosophers, it appears that neither of them had good taste in beer. The local beer I tasted in Jena was certainly not in the Bundesliga of Great German Beers. I was later ominously informed that it originated from the local hospice.)

Hegel arrived in Jena in 1801 and became a *privatdozent* at the university – a post where the pay depends upon the number of students who attend your lectures. Fortunately for Hegel, he had private means: at first only four students attended his lectures. (Unlike his great metaphysical predecessor Kant, whose literary style was execrable and lecturing style brilliant, Hegel preferred to be consistent: his lecturing style was as wretched as his literary style.)

At the end of the eighteenth century the University of Jena was the most exciting in Germany. Schiller delivered occasional lectures in history, the Schlegel brothers and the poet Novalis helped establish the first German romantic school there, and the latest post-Kantian philosophy was being expounded by the great Idealist Fichte. All these poetic figures had departed by the time Hegel arrived to lecture there, but in their place the twenty-six-year-old Schelling was inspiring students with the romantic enthusiasm of his nature philosophy. This was far too exciting for Hegel, and he soon began to fall out with Schelling.

Meanwhile, despite a dramatic increase in attendance at his lectures (to eleven), Hegel began to run out of money. But he refused to take the easy option. He had integrity like hedgehogs have prickles. Not for one moment was he tempted to make his lectures interesting or even comprehensible. Hegel was now beginning to formulate his great system, and he appears to have gradually worked it out as he went along – on his students. In the words of one of his later, admiring students: 'Stammering already at the beginning, he forced his way on, made a new beginning, again stopped short, spoke and meditated: the exact word seemed ever to be in request, and just then it came with infallible certainty ... Now, one felt one had grasped a proposition, and expected a further advance to be made. In vain. The thought, instead of advancing, kept turning with similar words again and again around the same point. Yet if the wearied attention was allowed to stray for a moment, one found on returning that one had lost the thread of discourse.' And remember, this is a description by a fervent disciple. We can only imagine the effect of this technique on the hapless student who had spent a night with the hospice beer.

So what could they do about Hegel? In the end someone appealed to Goethe, who was a privy councillor at the nearby court in Weimar and had influence with the authorities. Hegel was created an extraordinary professor (merely confirming the obvious, in the view of some of his colleagues) and granted a stipend of a hundred dollars.

This enabled Hegel to press on with his great philosophic work, *The Phenomenology of Mind*. But Hegel's phenomenal activities were not limited exclusively to the mind, for around this time his landlady became pregnant. This fact crops up in Hegel's biographies like the occasional rare gem of lucidity in his prose. One flash and it's gone, smothered in a welter of obfuscation. But this was no philosophical system where the truth can sometimes remain obscure until long after its author's demise. The landlady named Hegel as the culprit.

Napoleon was now gradually extending his domain over Europe. Conflict with Prussia became inevitable, and in 1806 French troops marched into Jena. Hegel despised Prussian bureaucracy and welcomed Napoleon. But this was not really a remnant of his youthful revolutionary fervour. Rather he felt he was witnessing the Process of History at work in accordance with his system. 'I saw Napoleon, that world soul, riding through the city.' Next day French soldiers began looting and setting fire to the houses in his street, and Hegel fled to the house of a nearby professor with the manuscript of *The Phenomenology of Mind* in his coat pocket. (Judging from the size of this work, he must have been wearing a *very* large coat.) Here Hegel completed the final sentences of his masterwork while the French and German armies battled outside the city. According to one story, when Hegel heard the soldiers returning he interrupted his work to peer out the window and ask, 'Who won?'

The French had won the Battle of Jena, and Hegel was overjoyed. The world soul was continuing its advance through the soulless world. But after the battle the university was forced to close down, and Hegel found himself practically broke again, reduced to living off his stipend. The following year *The Phenomenology of Mind* was published.

This book is generally considered to be Hegel's most masterful and complex work. Kant had already set eight hundred pages as the required length for a German philosophical text, and here Hegel showed he was up to the standard of his great predecessor. But where Hegel far outshone Kant was in the prolixity of his prose style. As an example I have purposely chosen one of his clearer, simpler sentences: 'Meanwhile, as mind itself is not an abstractly simple entity, but a system of processes, wherein it distinguishes itself into moments, but in the very act of distinguishing remains free and detached; and as mind articulates its body as a whole into a variety of functions, and designates one particular part of the body for only one function: so too one can represent to oneself the fluent state of its internal existence (its existence within itself) as something that is articulated into parts.' And so on . . .

This Matterhorn of a molehill may appear hilarious taken one sentence at a time. But after several hundred pages you may find the joke wearing thin.

Yet do not be deceived into thinking that the entire work is like this. Hegel gradually (*very* gradually) built up to a final apotheosis in which Absolute Knowledge was described. It's difficult even to conceive of a sentence of over half a dozen lines that remains throughout its entire length utterly bereft of meaning. (Just try.) But by now Hegel had the bit between his teeth and could manage it for pages on end: 'To know the pure notions of knowledge in the form in which they are modes or shapes of consciousness – this constitutes the aspect of their reality, according to which their essential element, the notion, appearing there in its simple mediating activity as thinking, breaks up and separates the moments of this mediation and exhibits them to itself in accordance with their immanent opposition.'

Hegel claimed this was 'an attempt to teach philosophy to speak German'. Some think he succeeded. But this mischievous view is an insult to German, the language of Hölderlin and Rilke. Before trying to teach philosophy anything, perhaps Hegel should have taught *himself* to speak German.

But what exactly does all this mean? One cannot produce an eight-hundred-page work in any language without it meaning something. Armed with this article of faith, many a scholar has ventured into the quagmire of Hegel's prose. Some have emerged as Marxists, others as existentialists, and still others have not emerged at all (the Hegelians). In the end it took Hegel ten volumes to *summarize* this philosophy. (The new definitive edition of his works by the Deutsche Forschungsgemeinschaft is expected to run to more than fifty volumes.) So any attempt to encapsulate Hegel's thought is like trying to infer, from the tiny bone at the tip of the dinosaur's tail, the huge, lumbering, extinct beast from which it originated.

In *The Phenomenology of Mind* Hegel describes the logical process by which the human mind rose from simple consciousness, through the stages of self-consciousness, reason, spirit, and religion, to Absolute Knowledge. This contains the blueprint upon which he was to base his greatest all-embracing system.

Hegel's system included absolutely everything. Whether it is right about absolutely everything (or indeed anything at all) depends upon how one regards its basic structure and dynamic. The entire system rests on Hegel's original mode of reasoning – his celebrated dialectical method. This starts with a 'thesis'. For example: Existence. According to Hegel, this is inevitably seen to be inadequate and incomplete. When we contemplate the notion 'existence', it generates its opposite, its 'antithesis': Nonexistence. This too is then seen to be inadequate, and the two opposites then merge to form a 'synthesis'. In this case: Becoming. This synthesis retains what is rational in both the thesis and the antithesis, and in its turn may become another thesis. This allows the process to be repeated, in a series of triads, ascending into ever more rational realms. As it becomes more rational, it becomes more spiritual. And as it becomes more spiritual, it becomes more conscious of itself and its own significance. This process arrives at Absolute Knowledge, which is 'spirit knowing itself as spirit'.

But the vital element of the system remains the dialectic, which operates at all levels, from the loftiest spiritual realms to the murkier processes of history, art, science, and so forth. An example of Hegel's dialectic at these levels is:

Thesis: Architecture.

Antithesis: The romantic arts.

Synthesis: Classical sculpture.

Whether or not the above argument bears any relation to the truth, as we see it, is not our concern for the moment. It is presented merely to illustrate Hegel's method and the sort of material he put through this universal mincer. A more vague, abstract example (to which, of course, the method was much more suited) is:

Thesis: Universality.

Antithesis: Particularity.

Synthesis: Individuality.

Hegel's dialectical method (which he referred to as logic) sprung from a laudable ambition. He wished to overcome the main deficiency of traditional logic – the fact that it was entirely vacuous. Logic never says anything about anything but itself. Take for instance a traditional argument such as:

All philosophers are intellectual megalomaniacs.

Hegel is a philosopher.

Therefore Hegel is an intellectual megalomaniac.

Logically this argument would be just the same if it were about wizards, magicians, and Merlin. So it could be written:

All A are B.

X is A.

Therefore X is B.

The *logical* form remains the same regardless of the content. According to Hegel, the aim of logic is truth. But if the truth is empty of content, what is it? Nothing. The empty truth of this traditional kind of logic gives no information. It cannot discover the actual truth. Hegel wished to overcome this separation of form and content.

His argument runs as follows, and he intended that it should be absorbed in its entirety. (Leaps of ordinary logic, which may defy our credulity, are resolved when the argument is viewed as a whole, we are assured.) Hegel begins by saying that logic is the study of thought. As we have seen, the dialectical process ascends towards mind or Absolute Spirit. Mind is the ultimate reality, abstracted from the particular forms it assumes in the natural world. It is mind that shapes the world. Therefore a study of how mind works (thought) will reveal how the world works.

From the above argument it follows that there is no objective reality independent of thought. Indeed, in *The Phenomenology of Mind* Hegel argues that thought is objective reality, and vice versa. The two are one and the same thing. This means that when logic is directed towards thought, it is also directed towards reality. The subject matter of logic is thus 'the truth as it is'.

So the dialectic – with its triadic method of thesis, antithesis, and synthesis – has both form and content. It 'works the way the mind works', and it deals with 'the truth as it is'. A thesis generates its antithesis through its formal inability to accommodate its content in its entirety. As in the thesis Existence, which necessarily generates its antithesis Nonexistence, with the two then merging to form their synthesis Becoming.

Undeniably this system generates a wide range of striking, profound, and thought-provoking ideas. But these remain essentially poetic. Indeed, the whole system is essentially a beautiful poetic idea. But this butterfly is pinned with a sledgehammer. And in many of the lower reaches of the pyramid the ideas are not only wrong (Thesis: The Jewish religion. Antithesis: The Roman religion. Synthesis: The Greek religion) but vacuous (Thesis: Air. Antithesis: Earth. Synthesis: Fire and water). From this it can be seen that despite Hegel's claim that his system is necessary (in the logical sense), it remains largely arbitrary. Its logic has none of the rigour of Spinoza's geometric system, for instance. And as we shall see, when it strays into more practical areas, such as history, it can generate some very nasty ideas indeed. (The notion of a national leader as the embodiment of the 'world soul' may have had some poetic justification in Napoleon's day but is definitely not acceptable thinking in the light of twentieth-century experience.)

Despite the publication of this gross work, Hegel was still broke. The university remained closed, and he began looking for a job. But by now a dialectical process closer to home had produced its inevitable synthesis: Hegel's landlady had given birth to a son, named Ludwig.

A short time later Hegel left Jena to take up the post of editor of the *Bamburger Zeitung*, a job he was to hold for the next two years. Alas, we can only imagine what his editorials were like, as all copies of this newspaper dating from 1807–1808 appear to have fallen foul of the spiritualising process of history.

At the age of thirty-eight Hegel now became headmaster of a *Gymnasium* in Nuremberg. This post he was to hold for the next eight years, and it gave him sufficient free time to continue with his philosophical work. By this time Hegel had long since abandoned the thesis of revolutionary liberation and had embraced its antithesis with a vengeance. He was perfect for the post of headmaster, declaring, 'The ideal of all education is to root up those individual imaginations, thoughts and reflections which youth may have and form ... Thought, as much as will, must commence with obedience.'

Like many schoolmasters who are uninterested in their job, or just plain lazy, he was a martinet. One disturbed Herr Rektor Hegel in his study at his peril. One of his pupils relates: 'I and another were sent along to lay the pupils' grievances before him. But what a reception we got! I scarcely knew how we got down the stairs.'

Then another amazing antithesis took place. Hegel fell in love. This concept may be as difficult for some to grasp as Hegel's dialectical notion of the Absolute. By now Hegel was forty years old and a confirmed bachelor (apart from one unfortunate lapse). Years of unremitting study had taken their toll. His sullen pasty face was prematurely aged, he had lank receding hair, and the portraits catch a distinct shiftiness in his eyes. He was thick-set but stooped, with a rather embarrassed, awkward social manner. Georg Wilhelm Friedrich Hegel appears to have had no charisma, even in the eyes of his most ardent disciples. The girl he fell in love with, Marie von Tucher, came from a respectable old Nuremberg family and was just eighteen years old.

Marie was a friend of Jean Paul, the popular early romantic novelist, and believed in such romantic notions as 'feeling' and impulsive gestures. Hegel wrote her lumbering poems in which he painstakingly analysed the dialectical nature of love. Even when they met on their trysts, Hegel remained very much the headmaster, often adoping a censorious tone with regard to Marie's flighty romantic notions. Afterwards, in his letters, he would attempt to apologise: 'I confess that when I have to condemn principles, I too early lose sight of the way and manner in which they are present in a particular individual – in this case, in you – and that I am apt to take them too earnestly because I see in them their universal bearing and consequence, which you do not think of – which, indeed, for you are not in them at all.' One wonders what he would have said if she'd planted a 'Tree of Liberty' in the marketplace, as Hegel had done at her age. But the fact is, Marie seems to have returned the love of her fuddy-duddy old sourpuss.

In 1811 they were married – a joyous social event which was slightly marred by the unexpected appearance of Hegel's Jena landlady, who created a scene. Indignantly she brandished a piece of paper which she claimed was Hegel's written promise to marry her. According to one report, she was 'appeased and indemnified'.

But another old flame was not so easily extinguished. When Hegel's sister Christiane heard of his marriage she had a nervous breakdown (described in the unfeeling chauvinist parlance of the time as 'hypochondriacal melancholy with outbursts of hysteria'). Christiane had been working as a governess and had not been able to bring herself to marry. Her rejection of one suitor had resulted in an outbreak of 'nervousness' accompanied by 'bizarre behaviour'. Hegel offered to take her in, but Christiane's violent jealousy of Hegel's wife made this offer unthinkable to her. Instead she went to stay with a relative, where to begin with she spent all day on the sofa howling and screaming. According to the relative, she expressed 'deep dissatisfaction' with her brother and 'deep hatred' of his wife. Her condition deteriorated to the point where she was confined in an asylum, but she was released after a year.

Hegel maintained his customary imperturbability, but this evidence of mental instability in his sister must surely have caused him alarm. He continued to suffer from bouts of deep depression, and at one stage he described a 'descent into dark regions where nothing shows itself to be firm, determinate, and secure, where splendours flash everywhere, but next to abysses'. He told how he first became aware of his philosophy, and suggested that 'every human being who has such a turning point' experiences 'the nocturnal point of the contraction of his nature through whose narrows he is pressed, fortified and assured to feel secure with himself and secure in the usual daily life; and if he has already rendered himself incapable of being satisfied with that, secure in an inner noble existence'. Psychiatrists have frequently pointed to the 'yearning for protection or safety . . . that animates so much even abstract thinking'. Hegel's philosophy, which came from a profound impulse, may well have reflected a deep internal division in his psyche. Such speculation would be open to ridicule were it not for the uncannily schizoid (and subsequent healing) nature of his dialectical process, which he saw as 'the way mind works'.

Despite all these difficulties, Hegel's marriage was by all accounts a happy one. Marie produced two sons, Karl and Immanuel. As they grew up they were joined by their third brother, Ludwig, who came to live with the family after the death of his mother in Jena. Despite Hegel's best intentions, this didn't work out. Ludwig was consumed with resentment. He appears to have inherited more than a little of his father's intellect. Following in his father's footsteps, he became a student radical. He wanted to study medicine, but Hegel insisted that he take up commerce. Ludwig ran away and joined the Dutch Foreign Legion; he was then shipped to the East Indies, where he caught fever and died.

It was during this period that Hegel wrote his second great work, *The Science of Logic*. This magniloqum opus is distinguished by being almost entirely devoid of the two subjects mentioned in its title. By science, Hegel meant metaphysics – the very antithesis of physics. And by logic he meant his dialectical method. If you accept Hegel's dialectical method as logical, his system is indeed the most rigidly structured, comprehensive, and brilliantly argued system ever conceived. If you don't accept this, there is a strong temptation to view the whole thing as a metaphysical aberration. (According to such a view, Hegel should have called this work *The Metaphysics of Metaphysics*, which would indeed have better indicated its contents.)

In *The Science of Logic* Hegel doesn't consider logic but instead considers the concepts we use when arguing logically – such as Kant's categories (being, quantity, relation, and so forth). Of these the most important for Hegel is relation, and the most universal relation is contradiction. Thus begins the dialectical process of thesis, antithesis, and synthesis. As we have already seen, Hegel considered thought as the ultimate reality, and as the dialectical method governed the process of thought, so it also governed reality. This, for Hegel, was the 'science' of his logic. Everything was subject to the dialectical method.

The Science of Logic reveals the fundamental difference between Kant and Hegel. Kant was fully qualified to write a book on science and logic, being an original scientist and a brilliant logician. Hegel, on the other hand, took the historical approach to philosophy. It's not just his sentences that take the long-term view on the outcome of events. Hegel saw the world comprehensively, as an ever-evolving historical process. Such a view blurs the particularity of the here and now. Everything stands in the shadows of historical perspective. By comparison, Kant viewed the world with the clarity of a scientist. Kant's view is the one in fashion at present, but with human history approaching the end of a long expansionist era, it's possible that Hegel's view may yet re-emerge.

The Science of Logic made Hegel famous. After only its first part was published, the universities of Heidelberg and Berlin offered him professorships. He chose Heidelberg, where he arrived in 1816. Hegel is the most prestigious philosopher to have held a post at this university during its long history, and on the hillside across the river from the city is a path known as the Philosopher's Walk. To reach this path you climb through vineyards: below is the old bridge across the Neckar, and on the far bank lies the centuries-old university city laid out beneath its castle. Years ago someone told me that the Philosopher's Walk was named after Hegel, but since then I've been told this isn't true, as Hegel apparently detested going for walks in the country.

A year after arriving in Heidelberg, Hegel published *The Encyclopedia of the Philosophical Sciences in Outline* for students to read before attending his lectures. This contains an outline of his entire philosophy and lets the reader in on the code of his jargon as well as his eccentric use of various words. Logic wasn't the only concept to suffer: by now his lectures were completely incomprehensible unless you were up on the gobbledygook. Even the simplest explanations needed decoding: 'If we review in brief the moments of this transition of Quality in to Quantity, the qualitative has for fundamental determination Being and immediacy, where limit and determinatedness are identical with the being of the Something in such a manner that, these being altered, the something itself vanishes.' (Not for nothing were several of those who broke the fiendishly difficult German Enigma code during World War II former Hegel students.)

In *The Encyclopedia of the Philosophical Sciences in Outline* Hegel also elaborates his system. This can be viewed as a series of pyramidal structures, culminating in a supertriad whose thesis is the Absolute Idea, which generates its antithesis Nature, and whose synthesis is Spirit or Absolute Reality. The entire system can be viewed as Spirit (which is also Absolute Reality) contemplating itself and its own significance. As individuals we gradually move up through this system as we become more rational, more mind, more conscious of ourselves and our significance.

This system is a vast spiritual monism – the all-embracing synthesis of the Absolute Idea and Nature: Spirit (or Absolute Reality). But besides being triadic, it can also be viewed as cyclical, for differentiation is a necessary part of this whole. The dialectical method operates throughout: thesis generating antithesis, and so on. Truth can only be known after it has differentiated itself – generated its antithesis, error – and overcome this. Likewise God is only infinite because He has taken on the limitation of the finite and overcome this. (A similar dialectical process is echoed in the fall of man, which was necessary so that he could achieve goodness.) As well as the integration of synthesis, there is always the differentiation of thesis generating antithesis.

In 1818 Hegel decided to embrace the antithesis of his decision to accept the post at Heidelberg: he now accepted the offer of a post at Berlin. Here he became professor of philosophy, the position that had become vacant on the death of Fichte. By now Napoleon had been defeated, and Prussia was once again the dominant German state. It was embarking upon its most stiflingly conservative era, and Berlin was its capital. Hegel was to remain in Berlin for the next thirteen years. His lectures became an institution, attracting hundreds of students, and the miasma of his philosophical influence began to spread throughout German universities in the form of Hegelianism.

Virtually all freedom of thought and political expression were forbidden in Prussia at the time. This meant that the intellectual energies of the students and sophisticated citizens of Berlin had to seek release elsewhere. The result was a great boom in the arts, philosophy, and music among the chattering classes.

Hegel became practically the official philosopher of the Prussian state. In 1821 he published *The Philosophy of Right*, which deals with politics and rights in society. Hegel was by now all in favour of the status quo and abhorred any thought of radical social change. The basic dialectic of his new work was:

Thesis: Abstract universal laws.

Antithesis: Personal conscience.

Synthesis: The ethics of a society.

Hegel believed that this society should rest on the values of the family and the established professions. Yet surprisingly, the state he envisaged is closer to the British model of the period than the Prussian. It included parliamentary government, a monarchy with limited powers, trial by jury, and toleration of dissent, especially of religious dissenters and Jews. (As far as I can discover, Hegel was entirely free of anti-Semitism, which was considered quite socially acceptable and reached epidemic proportions in Prussian society during this period.)

Meanwhile, Hegel continued doing what he knew best, bamboozling lecture halls filled with scores of earnest students. With his snuffbox laid out beside him on the lectern, and his large, lank-haired head bowed, he would shuffle awkwardly through his folios of notes, turning the pages forward and back as he hesitantly delivered sausagelike strings of abstruse qualifying clauses, his words frequently interrupted by bouts of coughing, until at last, rising to a plateau of pure abstraction, he would occasionally achieve an apotheosis of unexpected eloquence which momentarily lifted his speech above the constantly conflicting theses and antitheses of jargon to a sublime pinnacle transcending all meaning, where it would expand, as if of its own accord, before bursting into yet another fit of coughing.

Sometimes a particularly bamboozled student would afterward follow him to his rooms. Here he would find an odd, pasty-faced figure seated at a huge desk in a 'yellow-grey' dressing gown which reached to the floor, fumbling through scattered piles of discarded papers and books. In the midst of his awkward discourse with his visitor, the philosopher would often drift off, mumbling and fumbling for minutes on end, to all intents and purposes entirely oblivious of the other's presence.

Hegel published little during this period, but a number of dedicated cryptographers took notes at his lectures, and these have been published among his collected works. These published notes contain Hegel's most detailed exposition of his ideas on aesthetics, the philosophy of religion, and his notorious philosophy of history. This attempts to reduce history to a dialectic process – a pseudo-idea which was to return with a vengeance in the works of his follower Marx. According to this approach, history has a purpose (God's will for Hegel, the achievement of a Communist utopia for Marx). Hegel traces the crablike dialectic advance of history across the sand castles of time. The empires of China, ancient Greece, and Rome finally give way to the glories of the Prussian state, the highest form of community life ever known on earth (far transcending the rights of any mere individual). 'History shows us that when all but the name of philosophy was lost in other lands, it maintained itself as the peculiar possession of the German nation. We have received from Nature the high calling to be guardians of this sacred fire – as in earliest times the world-spirit maintained the highest consciousness in the Jewish nation.' It wasn't Hegel's idea that the earlier guardians of the sacred fire of highest consciousness should suffer the fate they did at the hands of the Nazis in the twentieth century. Hegel would have been appalled by Hitler and the abominations of the Third Reich. But writing such garbage didn't help matters, to say the least.

Hegel saw history from the widest possible perspective: a 'world-historical view'. History was viewed as a process of self-realisation. Humanity was embarked upon a journey of intellectual reflection and self-understanding, a growing awareness of its own unity and purpose. We take possession of our entire past when we see the story of our self-realisation as a meaningful whole, Hegel declared. So the aim of history was the discovery of the meaning of life, no less.

Progress, 'understanding the past' (as if it had only one interpretation), the meaning of life – far from being a 'world-historical view', such ideas are very much rooted to their time and place: early nineteenth-century Germany. The German states were uniting to become a powerful European nation; the Industrial Revolution was spreading throughout Europe; the world was entering a golden era of scientific discovery; and the European empires were spreading to the farthest outposts of the globe. It all looks very different from a late-twentieth-century perspective. 'Progress' is no longer regarded as inevitable, and humanity has even come to terms with the possibility of its own extinction. Likewise it is science that has taken on the lineaments of the Absolute, rather than Spirit. The Hegelian theory of history couldn't cope with such developments (any more than the system to which it gave birth, the Marxist theory of history, was able to cope with 'the inevitable collapse of the capitalist system' that obstinately refused to happen). We no longer view history as a meaningful and predetermined pattern but more as a scientific experiment whose outcome now lies largely in our hands.

Yet for all its faults, Hegel's view of history did not entirely cloud his judgment. Almost alone among nineteenth-century thinkers, he recognised the coming significance of America. 'In the era to come, this is where the burden of the world's history will reveal itself.' Marx, Nietzsche, Jules Verne – all the great nineteenth-century prophets missed the most significant development of the twentieth century.

In 1830 Hegel was appointed rector of Berlin University, and a year later he was decorated by King Frederick William III. But the antics of the world-spirit were now beginning to worry Hegel. In 1830 another revolt occurred in Paris, and this time Hegel wasn't out in the marketplace planting a 'Tree of Liberty'. When a ripple of this revolt spread to Berlin and prompted a popular uprising, Hegel became ill at the thought of mob rule. A year later he wrote an article in the *Preussische Staatszeitung* (*Prussian State Times*) criticising the Reform Bill that was then passing through the British parliament and airing his views on British democracy. In Hegel's view the British constitution was simply a shambles, he observed, compared with the 'rational institutions' of the Prussian state. And popular government, even the severely limited form practiced in Britain at the time, was a distinct impediment to the waltz-time dance of the world-spirit. (The Blue Dialectic). A government should not even try to express the will of the people. 'The people never knows what it wills.' But even this was far too revolutionary for the Prussian authorities, and the second instalment of Hegel's article was censored.

In 1831 Berlin suffered from the cholera epidemic that was raging through Germany, and Hegel moved out of town for the summer to a house in the nearby countryside. But nothing, not even cholera, could keep him from his beloved lecture hall. In November he returned to the city and delivered his first two days' lectures 'with a fire and energy of expression which surprised his hearers'. (His biographer Rosenkranz put this uncharacteristic eloquence down to the initial effects of cholera.) On the third day Hegel succumbed to the disease, and the day after, on 14 November 1831, he died peacefully in his sleep, unaware even that his life was in danger. He was buried, as he had wished, beside Fichte. His tomb, which can be seen in the Dorotheenstadt cemetery, just north of the city centre, is now regarded as a national shrine.

As soon as Hegel's sister Christiane heard of his death, she began writing a memoir describing their childhood together. This she sent to Hegel's widow, and some time afterwards drowned herself by walking into a river.

Five years later Karl Marx arrived as a student in Berlin and was introduced to the work of Hegel. After absorbing the main thesis of Hegel's ideas, and then reacting against them, he synthesised his philosophy of dialectical materialism – not at all what Hegel had had in mind for the world-spirit.

AFTERWORD

Hegel wished to be taken very seriously, and his wish came true. All over Europe the philosophical antidote of Hegelianism spread, rendering entire university philosophy departments immune from philosophical thinking. Hegelianism, with its enshrinement of the status quo, was just what was needed in Wilhelmine Germany and Victorian Britain. Such a glorious obfuscatory paean to the bourgeois state would surely have had to be invented if Hegel hadn't taken the immense trouble of creating it. Hegel's philosophy fulfilled all the requirements of the age. Discipline and order, a belief in hard work for its own sake, the improving nature of suffering, faith in a rigid system whose metaphysical foundations remained beyond all comprehension – all these were required of Hegel's readers (to say nothing of the late-nineteenth-century middle classes). Hegel's profound, all-embracing system resembled a colossal glass bead game: an intellectual challenge attracting many of the greatest minds of the time. And so it might conceivably have remained. But Europe was not about to enter the long stability of another mediaeval era, where the dialectic would take on an even greater role in thought than in syllogism.

Or was it? Attempts were certainly made – in differing forms yet with similarly horrific results – to institute such an era. Yet the blame for these monstrosities cannot be laid at the study door of the lonely professor in his yellow-grey dressing gown. His crime against language was obfuscation, theirs was lies. His understanding of the world was ultimately a stupendous intellectual fairy tale; they chose not even to try to understand the world, but to change it.

Hegelianism has been seen as an immensely elaborated Platonism. Plato believed in the ultimate reality of abstract ideas rather than the messy world of particulars which we appear to inhabit. The world we see around us is only real in so far as it partakes of these transcendent ideas. (For example, a red ball partakes of the abstract ideas of redness, roundness, elasticity, and so forth.) But in Hegelianism this simple melody of Platonic ideas was transformed into an interminable Wagnerian opera-cycle of bombast.

Ironically, all this may not have been a complete waste of time. Such grandiose metaphysical systems may have unwittingly served a historical purpose. The intricate techniques of the alchemists were similarly infused with metaphysics and intellectual whimsy, but they are now seen to have kept alive and developed the ideas that were to become chemistry. A similar process may well have been at work in nineteenth-century philosophy – with its vast metaphysical systems keeping alive and developing humanity's most ambitious intellectual project: a total systematic explanation of the world. The intellectual alchemy necessary for such a project continued to develop while modern science was in its infancy and incapable of such ambitions. But eventually plausibility prevailed. And now, instead of the dialectical method metamorphosing base arguments into gold, we have come to place our faith in the rickety and explosive apparatus of science.

Hegelianism's hubris was its claim to scientific rigour. As we have seen, the dialectical method was neither logical nor scientific. But even worse was Hegelianism's belief in an Absolute 'based on the structure of science'. The notion that this Absolute was the only ultimate reality led to a dangerous downgrading of the real world and those who inhabit it. The individual became something that 'didn't really exist' but was only part of a process that transcended him. The plagues of the twentieth century were political, and belief in this suicidal notion was to be their bacillus.

FROM HEGEL'S WRITINGS

All the rational is real and all the real is rational.

> – *The Philosophy of Right*, Preface

It is possible to show that the notion of philosophy is implicit even in our everyday thinking. We begin with our immediate perceptions and desires, but these soon urge us beyond their immediacy towards the apprehension of something greater than ourselves – an infinite being and infinite will. This is the course I have pursued in *The Phenomenology of Mind*.

> – *The Encyclopedia of the Philosophical Sciences in Outline*, 3

Time, like space, is a pure form of sensuous perception or institution. It is the condition of all immediate active perception, as well as that which is perceived i.e. of all experience, and all which is experienced. Nature is made of space and time, and is a process. When we stress its spatial aspect, we are aware of its objective nature; when we stress its temporal aspect, we become aware of its subjective nature. As we perceive it, nature is an unending and continuous process of becoming. Things arrive and depart within time. Such things are not only within time, but they are also temporal – time is a way of existing.

– *The Encyclopedia of the Philosophical Sciences in Outline*, 201

Every true or real logical thought has three aspects. Firstly, the abstract or comprehensible aspect, which indicates what a thing is. Secondly, its dialectical negation, which says what it is not. Thirdly, the speculative – which is concrete comprehension: A is at the same time that which it is not. These three aspects do not constitute the three aspects of logic; rather, they are moments of everything which has logical reality and truth. They are part of every philosophical concept. Every concept is rational, is an abstraction opposed to another, and is comprehended by a unity with its opposite. *This is the definition of the dialectic.*

– *The Encyclopedia of the Philosophical Sciences in Outline*, 13

All science, apart from philosophy, deals with objects which are taken for granted. The items under investigation are simply accepted prior to their scientific investigation. Likewise, interpretations gathered in this way are verified by referring back to the given material. Sciences have no need to justify the status of their material. Mathematics, jurisprudence, medicine, zoology, botany and so forth naturally presuppose the existence of magnitude, space, number, right, sickness, animals, plants, etc. . . .

With philosophy it is different. Philosophy begins in doubt and argument. It opens with a question about itself . . .

The object and method of philosophy are not assumed or agreed before we start philosophising. Investigating these things is what philosophy is about. This is what is so problematic about the subject. On the one hand, philosophy must begin by investigating itself; and on the other it must mediate with the world. This necessary uniting of the immediate and the mediate is what philosophy is.

> – *The Encyclopedia of the Philosophical Sciences in Outline*, 1, 2, 3

Experience and history teach us this: that nations and governments have never learned a thing from history, or acted in accordance with anything they might have learned from it.

> – *Lectures on the Philosophy of World History*, Introduction

So to be independent of public opinion is the first formal condition of achieving anything great or rational, either in life or science. Such achievement will assuredly be recognised in time by public opinion, which will duly transform it into one of its own prejudices.

> – *The Philosophy of Right*, 318

As a form of universal family, civil society has the right and duty to supervise and influence education, for education moulds a child's ability to become a member of society. In this instance society's right is of far more importance than the arbitrary and contingent wishes of the parents, especially where this education is to be completed not by the parents but by others.

– *The Philosophy of Right*, 239

We Germans would be Hegelians even if Hegel had never existed, in so far as, unlike the Mediterraneans, we instinctively attribute a deeper meaning and greater value to becoming and development, rather than to what is. We scarcely believe in the justification of the concept of being.

– Nietzsche, *Gay Science*, Aphorism 357

How will your free if not anarchic nature accept the Spanish torture of the method within which I confine Spirit?

– Letter 167 to von Sinclair (draft), mid-October 1810

In so far as philosophy may claim to be of independent interest, indeed even of the highest interest, its teacher must openly admit to everyone that nowhere can it be of much value except to a few.

– Letter 152 to van Ghert, Nuremberg, 16 December 1809

Only within the confines of the state does man have a rational existence. The aim of all education is to make sure that the individual ceases to remain purely subjective and attains an objective existence within the state ... He owes his entire existence to the state ... Whatever worth and spiritual reality he has are only as a result of the state.

– *Lectures on the Philosophy of World History*,
Introduction

In history we are concerned with what has been and what is; in philosophy, on the other hand, we are concerned not with what belongs exclusively to the past or even the future, but with what *is*, both now and eternally – that is, with reason.

– *Lectures on the Philosophy of World History*,
Introduction

The ethical order of society reached its goal and truth in the spirit that passed away within it – that is, the individual. However, this legal entity (a person) has its substance and fulfilment apart from the ethical order. The process of world culture and belief disposes of such an abstraction as a mere person; and by the completion of this process of estrangement, by attaining the extremity of abstraction, the self of spirit finds the substance become first the universal will, and finally its own possession. At this point knowledge at last appears to have become entirely adequate to the truth which is its goal; for its truth is this knowledge itself. Every opposition between the two sides has been eliminated, yet not for *us* (who are merely outlining the process), not merely *implicitly*, but actually for self-consciousness itself. Thus self-consciousness has mastered the opposition which consciousness itself involves. This opposition is the conflict between certainty of self and the object. But now the object for it *is* the certainty of self, which is knowledge: just as the certainty of itself as such no longer has ends of its own, is no longer conditioned and determinate, but is pure knowledge.

– *The Phenomenology of Mind*, Spirit, VI

The universal mind manifests itself in art as intuition and imagery, in religion it manifests itself as feeling and representative thinking, and in philosophy it occurs as pure freedom of thought. In world history the universal mind manifests itself as the actuality of mind in its entirety of internality and externality. World history is a court of judgment because in its absolute universality, the particular – that is, the forms of worship, society, and national minds in all the different actualities – is present only as ideal, and the movement of mind here is the manifestation of this . . .

World history is not the verdict of might – that is, of a blind destiny fulfilling itself in abstract and nonrational inevitability. On the contrary, because mind is implicitly and actually reason, and reason is explicit to itself in mind as knowledge, world history is the necessary development, out of the freedom of mind, of the moments of reason, and thus of the self-consciousness and freedom of mind.

The history of mind is its own action. Mind is only what it does, and its action makes itself the object of its own consciousness. Through history its action gains consciousness of itself as mind, it apprehends itself in its interpretation of itself to itself. This apprehension is its being and its principle, and the fulfilment of this apprehension at one stage is simultaneously the rejection of that stage and its elevation to a higher stage.

– *The Philosophy of Right*, World History

There are pages of Hegel which have the same effect in the realm of thought as the sonnets of Mallarmé have in the realm of poetry. They are vehicles of evocation and of vague sentimental nuances – nothing more. This does not belittle their value; it may even increase it. Yet verbal narcotics and hypnotic formulations should not be imposed on us as truths.

– Giovanni Papini, *Four and Twenty Minds*

When the Jesuits and Catholic missionaries first set out to teach the Indians European culture and manners . . . they went among the tribes and laid down daily routines for them as if they were schoolchildren; and no matter how idle the natives were, they duly obeyed. The missionaries also built storehouses, and showed the Indians how to use them, so that they could provide for their future needs. The missionaries chose the best methods of civilising their charges, treating them much as if they were children. I even recall that one missionary used to ring a bell at midnight to remind them to perform their marital duties, because otherwise it would never have occurred to them to do so. These rules initially had the (highly beneficial) effect of arousing their needs, these being the origin of all human activity.

– *Lectures on the Philosophy of World History*,
Introduction, Appendix 1

CHRONOLOGY OF SIGNIFICANT PHILOSOPHICAL DATES

6th C B.C.	The beginning of Western philosophy with Thales of Miletus.
End of 6th C B.C.	Death of Pythagoras.
399 B.C.	Socrates sentenced to death in Athens.
c 387 B.C.	Plato founds the Academy in Athens, the first university.
335 B.C.	Aristotle founds the Lyceum in Athens, a rival school to the Academy.
324 A.D.	Emperor Constantine moves capital of Roman Empire to Byzantium.
400 A.D.	St Augustine writes his *Confessions*. Philosophy absorbed into Christian theology.
410 A.D.	Sack of Rome by Visigoths heralds opening of Dark Ages.
529 A.D.	Closure of Academy in Athens by Emperor Justinian marks end of Hellenic thought.
Mid-13th C	Thomas Aquinas writes his commentaries on Aristotle. Era of Scholasticism.

1453	Fall of Byzantium to Turks, end of Byzantine Empire.
1492	Columbus reaches America. Renaissance in Florence and revival of interest in Greek learning.
1543	Copernicus publishes *On the Revolution of the Celestial Orbs*, proving mathematically that the earth revolves around the sun.
1633	Galileo forced by church to recant heliocentric theory of the universe.
1641	Descartes publishes his *Meditations*, the start of modern philosophy.
1677	Death of Spinoza allows publication of his *Ethics*.
1687	Newton publishes *Principia*, introducing concept of gravity.
1689	Locke publishes *Essay Concerning Human Understanding*. Start of empiricism.
1710	Berkeley publishes *Principles of Human Knowledge*, advancing empiricism to new extremes.
1716	Death of Leibniz.
1739–1740	Hume publishes *Treatise of Human Nature*, taking empiricism to its logical limits.
1781	Kant, awakened from his 'dogmatic slumbers' by Hume, publishes *Critique of Pure Reason*. Great era of German metaphysics begins.

1807	Hegel publishes *The Phenomenology of Mind*, high point of German metaphysics.
1818	Schopenhauer publishes *The World as Will and Representation*, introducing Indian philosophy into German metaphysics.
1889	Nietzsche, having declared 'God is dead', succumbs to madness in Turin.
1921	Wittgenstein publishes *Tractatus Logico-Philosophicus*, claiming the 'final solution' to the problems of philosophy.
1920s	Vienna Circle propounds Logical Positivism.
1927	Heidegger publishes *Being and Time*, heralding split between analytical and Continental philosophy.
1943	Sartre publishes *Being and Nothingness*, advancing Heidegger's thought and instigating existentialism.
1953	Posthumous publication of Wittgenstein's *Philosophical Investigations*. High era of linguistic analysis.

CHRONOLOGY OF HEGEL'S LIFE

1770	Born 27 August in Stuttgart.
1781	Has severe bout of fever, which also strikes his entire family, resulting in the death of his mother.
1788	Studies theology at Tübingen University, where he meets Hölderlin and Schelling.
1793	After graduating from Tübingen, moves to Berne in Switzerland to take up post as private tutor.
1796	Hölderlin secures him a tutoring post in Frankfurt.
1799	Death of Hegel's father leaves him with a small private income.
1801	With the aid of Schelling, appointed as *privatdozent* (junior lecturer) at Jena University.
1806	Hegel finishes *The Phenomenology of Mind* as Napoleon wins Battle of Jena.
1807	Becomes editor of the *Bamberger Zeitung*.
1808	Becomes headmaster of *Gymnasium* in Nuremberg.
1811	Marries Marie von Tucher.

1812	Publishes first part of *The Science of Logic*, completed four years later.
1817	Publishes *The Encyclopedia of the Philosophical Sciences in Outline*.
1818	Becomes professor of philosophy at University of Berlin.
1821	Publishes *The Philosophy of Right*.
1830	Deeply upset by riots in Berlin. Appointed rector of the University of Berlin.
1831	Dies of cholera in Berlin on 14 November.

CHRONOLOGY OF HEGEL'S ERA

1770	Birth of Hölderlin, Beethoven, and Wordsworth.
1776	American colonies achieve independence from Great Britain: birth of the United States of America.
1786	Death of Frederick the Great.
1789	French Revolution.
1793	French Revolution develops into the Terror under Robespierre.
1806	Napoleon wins Battle of Jena.
1813	Birth of Wagner. Napoleon defeated at Battle of Waterloo and consequently exiled to St Helena. British consolidate empire over whole of India.
1819	Simon Bolivar launches his campaign to rid South America of Spanish colonial rule.
1821	Faraday discovers principle of the electric motor.
1825	Birth of the railway: Stockton to Darlington route opened by Stephenson.
1829	British annex whole of Australian subcontinent.

1830	Greece achieves independence from Ottoman Empire.
1831	Darwin sets sail on *HMS Beagle* for Galápagos Islands.
1832	Death of Goethe in Weimar.

RECOMMENDED READING

G. W. F. Hegel, *Lectures on the History of Philosophy*, Vol. 3, *Medieval and Modern Philosophy*, edited by Robert F. Brown (University of California Press, 1990).

Michael J. Inwood, *A Hegel Dictionary* (Blackwell, 1992).

Terry Pinkard, *Hegel's Phenomenology: The Sociality of Reason* (Cambridge University Press, 1994).

Robert S. Pippin, *Hegel's Idealism: The Satisfactions of Self-Consciousness* (Cambridge University Press, 1989).

Peter Singer, *Hegel* (Oxford University Press, 1983).

INDEX

A NOTE ON THE AUTHOR

PAUL STRATHERN was educated at Trinity College, Dublin, and lectures in mathematics and philosophy at Kingston University. He has written five novels, one of which won a Somerset Maugham Prize. His most recent works include *Dr Strangelove's Game: A Brief History of Economic Genius* and *Mendeleyev's Dream: The Quest for the Elements*, which was shortlisted for the Aventis Science Prize. He has also written for many journals including the *Observer* (London), *Wall Street Journal* and *New Scientist*. His popular Philosophers in 90 Minutes series is being published worldwide in fifteen languages.